PROPERTY OF
OF EDUCATION
RILL SCHOOL

MORRILL ELEMENTARY SCHOOL

3488000816871

W9-ATR-959

921
Jor

C i l

Roberts, Naurice.

Barbara Jordan, the
great lady from Texas

DATE DUE

PROPERTY OF
CHICAGO BOARD OF EDUCATION
DONALD L. MORRILL SCHOOL

BARBARA JORDAN
The Great Lady
From Texas

by Naurice Roberts

 CHILDRENS PRESS, CHICAGO

Picture Acknowledgments

Black Star — © 1983 Nancy Schiff, 2;
                    © Dennis Black, 14 (right), 22

Wide World Photos — 6, 8, 11 (two photos), 18, 19, 20 (left), 25, 26, 27, 31

United Press International — 16 (two photos), 22, 23, 24

News & Information Service, University of Texas at Austin — cover, 13, 28, 29

Library of Congress Cataloging-in-Publication Data

Roberts, Naurice.
    Barbara Jordan, the great lady from Texas.

    Summary: A biography of the Texas lawyer and teacher
who, among other achievements, served three terms in the
House of Representatives, the first black woman ever to
be elected to that office from the South.
    1. Jordan, Barbara, 1936-   —Juvenile literature.
2. Legislators — United States — Biography — Juvenile literature.   3. United States.   Congress.   House — Biography
—Juvenile literature. [1. Jordan, Barbara, 1936-
2. Legislators   3. Lawyers   4. Afro-Americans — Biography]
I. Title.
E840.8.J62R62   1984   328.73'092'4   [B]   [92] 83-23158
ISBN 0-516-03511-8

Copyright © 1990, 1984 by Childrens Press®, Inc.
All rights reserved. Published simultaneously in Canada.
Printed in the United States of America.

7   8   9   10   R   93   92   91   90

BARBARA JORDAN
The Great Lady
From Texas

When Barbara Jordan was sworn in as governor of Texas, she became the first black woman in the history of the United States to hold this office even for a single day.

She stood tall and straight with her head held high and proud. She raised her right hand and promised to uphold the Texas Constitution. Everyone clapped and cheered.

On June 10, 1972, when both Texas Governor Preston Smith and Lieutenant Governor Ben Barnes were out of the state for a day, Barbara Jordan, as *president pro tempore* (temporary president) of the state senate, became the first black to serve as governor of Texas.

Some people thought it was silly for a person to be sworn in as governor of Texas for just one day. But Barbara Jordan didn't think so.

“Someday,” she told reporters
who covered the swearing-in
ceremony, “I may want to retain the
governor’s seat for a longer period
of time.”

Everyone in Texas believed that
Barbara Jordan could really do it if
she wanted to. That’s because she
always wanted to be something
special. Even as a little girl.

Barbara Charline Jordan was born in Houston, Texas, on February 21, 1936. She was the third and youngest daughter of the Reverend Benjamin and Arlynne Jordan. The Jordan family lived in a nice, neat house in Houston's poor black community.

Barbara's parents believed in strict discipline, especially her father, who was a Baptist minister.

She and her sisters, Bennie and Rose Mary, were taught respect, dignity, and self-worth. They learned the value of hard work and study. Their father always said they could be anything in life. But they had to work hard.

And Barbara did work hard. She was nearly a straight A student. Once she received a B. She wasn't very happy. So, Barbara worked to develop "brain power." As her father would say, "No one could ever take away your brains!"

There was fun, too. People walking past the Jordan home at 4910 Campbell Street often could hear music. Almost everyone played an instrument. Barbara's favorite was the guitar.

But living in the South was not always fun for thousands of black people. Barbara understood this. She knew that a black must be well educated. It was the only way to get ahead.

In the segregated South blacks were not allowed to go to the same school or even eat at the same lunch counters as whites. In the 1960s civil rights workers changed these laws. In peaceful demonstrations they integrated lunch counters (left), buses, and schools. They often had to face hostile crowds, such as the one shown above, but they did not weaken. Today these segregation laws have been overturned by the Supreme Court of the United States.

When Barbara was in the tenth grade, she heard a speech by a black lawyer from Chicago. She was very impressed. She decided to be a lawyer just like Edith Spurlock Sampson. Miss Sampson later became a circuit court judge in Illinois.

Barbara had a burning desire to excel. She was serious and determined to succeed.

In 1952, Barbara graduated at the top of her class from Phyllis Wheatley High School. That fall she enrolled in Texas Southern University, an all-black school in Houston, Texas. There she became a campus leader, scholar, and debate champion.

Debating was one of her favorite activities. Barbara was an excellent speaker and had an extensive

Professor Jordan leads a discussion group at the Lyndon Baines Johnson School of Public Affairs.

vocabulary. She enjoyed talking about a subject in public with someone who had a different opinion. Her strong, clear voice would fill the room. Everyone watched her and listened to each word. Barbara and her debating team won many awards and honors. In 1956, she graduated with a bachelor of arts degree in history and political science, *magna cum laude*, a high honor in college.

Barbara studied law at Boston
University in Boston, Massachusetts.
Things were different in this city.
Barbara could go anywhere she
wanted. This was not like Texas,
where blacks and whites went to
separate places.

After graduation from law school
in 1959, Barbara could have stayed
in Boston and enjoyed an easy life.
But she decided to return home.
The civil rights movement had
started. Many blacks and whites
were working together to end

segregation. They were working to make certain the law would be equal for everyone, black or white. Barbara Jordan wanted to take part in this struggle. As a lawyer, she knew she could help change things.

Starting a law practice was not easy. There was very little money. So the young lawyer turned the family dining room into an office. Things were slow at first, but they soon began to pick up.

Barbara still wanted to change things for black people. She decided the best way to do it was through politics. It was 1960, an election year. The vice-presidential candidate was from Texas. His name was Lyndon Baines Johnson. He would soon become a good friend to Barbara.

Vice President Lyndon Baines Johnson (left) and President John F. Kennedy (right) applaud as parade units pass their stand on inauguration day in 1961.

In 1969 President Johnson was the first outgoing president in 169 years to personally deliver his State of the Union address to a joint session of Congress.

The young lawyer proved to be a very good worker. People enjoyed her speeches. They liked to hear her talk. Barbara convinced everyone that voting was important.

The election was successful. John F. Kennedy was elected president and Lyndon Baines Johnson, vice-president. Barbara felt proud. She had helped a fellow Texan become vice-president of the United States.

The smart lawyer continued to work for political and civic causes.

More and more people knew who Barbara Jordan was and what things she believed in. Soon she decided to run for the Texas state senate. This was very unusual. No black had been elected to the house of representatives since the days of Reconstruction, after the Civil War. Barbara ran, but 1962 was not the right time. She lost. Not happy with defeat, she tried again in 1964. She lost again to the same opponent.

Defeat was depressing. Barbara thought about leaving Texas and going where blacks in politics would be accepted. But she said, "I'm a Texan. To leave would be a cop-out!" She decided to stay in Houston.

Barbara Jordan, 1967.

   Judge Bill Elliott had been
watching Barbara's work. He knew
she was smart so he asked Barbara
to be his assistant. This was the first
time a black was appointed to such
a high office in Houston. The job
was working with needy people.

   Although Barbara liked her work,
she liked politics, too. She decided
to run for the state senate. This time
things were a lot different. She won!
On May 27, 1967, Barbara Jordan
was sworn in as the first black state

State Senator Barbara Jordan spoke at the
National Black Political Convention in 1972.

senator since 1883. She was only
thirty-one years old. It was a very
proud moment.

The black woman senator from
Houston was soon the most popular
senator in the state. She worked to
end discrimination. She worked on
laws that gave farm workers and
others the right to earn a minimum
wage. Her fellow senators respected
and admired her so much they paid
her a rare tribute by recognizing her
outstanding work as a freshman
senator. The city of Houston

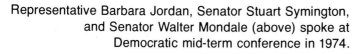
Representative Barbara Jordan, Senator Stuart Symington, and Senator Walter Mondale (above) spoke at Democratic mid-term conference in 1974.

honored her, too. Mayor Louie Welch proclaimed October 1, 1971, as Barbara Jordan Day.

In 1972, State Senator Barbara Jordan had been elected *president pro tempore* (temporary president) of the senate. She would take over if the governor or lieutenant governor were out of the state. The day they both were, Barbara was sworn in as governor. She was the first black woman in United States history to be governor — even for one day.

Now, everyone was watching this great Texas state senator. When Barbara announced she would run for Congress, no one was surprised. She received a great deal of help from friends, including the former president of the United States, Lyndon Baines Johnson. Johnson liked Barbara very much. They were good friends. In 1972 she was elected to the U.S. House of Representatives. Then it was off to Washington, D.C., the nation's capital. She was the first black woman from a southern state to serve in Congress.

From left to right: Martha Griffiths (Michigan), Shirley Chisholm (New York), Elizabeth Holtzman (New York), Barbara Jordan (Texas), Yvonne Brathwaite Burke (California), and Bella Abzug (New York) were members of the House of Representatives in 1973.

Congress was not like the Texas state senate. The freshman lawmaker had a lot to learn. She spent many hours reading and studying. There were meetings and conferences to attend. Soon, Barbara Jordan was an outstanding legislator just as she had been in Texas. She also became a member of the Congressional Black Caucus, a group of black legislators.

Congresswoman Jordan felt strongly about the law and the

Barbara Jordan,
Peter Rodino,
and John Doar
were on the House
Judiciary Committee.

Constitution. She believed the law
should work for all Americans. No
one was above the law.

In 1974, Barbara was part
of a committee that was meeting
to decide if the president of the
United States, Richard Nixon, had
covered-up the fact that some of his
aides had broken the law. For
months the entire country watched
the gentle lady from Texas. Her
powerful voice was heard on radio

President Richard M. Nixon resigned from office on August 8, 1974.

and television. Reporters wrote about her in newspapers and magazines. In July of 1974 the committee voted. They said that because of the facts they had collected in their hearings the president should be charged with breaking the law.

But before the full House of Representatives could act on the recommendations of the committee, President Nixon resigned. The day Nixon left the White House was a sad one in American history.

Representative Barbara Jordan congratulates President Gerald Ford after he signed a fair trade law for consumers.

The new president, Gerald Ford, had great respect for Barbara Jordan. In 1974 he asked her to be one of his personal representatives to Peking, China.

By now, Congresswoman Jordan was a popular national figure. She was selected Democratic Woman of the Year by the Women's National Democratic Club. The *Ladies' Home Journal* named her their Woman of the Year in politics. *Time* magazine

Barbara acknowledges the applause after giving her
speech at the Democratic National Convention in 1976.

made her Woman of the Year and in
a *Redbook* magazine survey she was
named a Woman Who Could Be
President.

In 1976, millions of people across
the country saw and heard Barbara
Jordan give what some considered
the most dynamic speech of her
career at the Democratic National

President Jimmy Carter and Barbara Jordan
at the Democratic National Convention in 1976.

Convention in New York. She
received a standing ovation. People
were cheering, shouting, and even
crying. Many thought she would be
a good candidate for vice-president
of the United States. But the
outstanding legislator liked her job
in Congress and decided to stay
where she was.

In 1978, after serving three terms
in the House of Representatives,
Barbara Jordan retired from public

The Lyndon Baines Johnson School of Public Affairs is in
Richardson Hall (right), and the Lyndon Baines Johnson Library
and Museum (center) at the University of Texas at Austin.

office and returned to Houston.
Since that time she has been a
Public Service Professor at the
Lyndon Baines Johnson School of
Public Affairs at the University of
Texas in Austin.

In 1982 she was appointed to a
special place of honor called the
Lyndon Baines Johnson Centennial
Chair in National Policy at the
university. She directs a research
program on national policy issues
and concerns.

Professor Jordan with some of her students

Thousands of students have heard the former congresswoman lecture about important national issues and her experiences as a public servant. Professor Jordan enjoys teaching. "I'm learning, and the students and I are learning together," she said.

Although she still works hard, things are not as hectic as they were when she was in public office.

Barbara Jordan continues to write as well as lecture. One of her special concerns is the issue of ethics in public life. She has written a book about her life experiences. She has also been on television as a commentator.

Professor Jordan also keeps up with her favorite football teams. She is a great fan of the Dallas Cowboys and the Houston Oilers.

Barbara Jordan returned to the national political scene on July 21, 1988, when she gave a speech at the Democratic National Convention in Atlanta, Georgia. She seconded the nomination of Senator Lloyd Bentsen of Texas for Democratic vice-presidential candidate.

In 1977, Barbara received an honorary doctor of laws degree from Harvard University.

Barbara Jordan is still one of America's most admired public figures. Some say she could have been an excellent cabinet member, an ambassador, a Supreme Court justice, or even president of the United States.

Perhaps one day she will hold one of these positions. If she does, she will again prove to the world that someone with "brain power" and the willingness to work hard can indeed make history.

BARBARA CHARLINE JORDAN

1936   Born February 21, Houston, Texas
1956   Graduated *magna cum laude* from Texas Southern University
1959   Graduated from Boston University Law School
1966   Elected as first black state senator since 1883
1972   Governor for one day, June 10; elected to United States House of Representatives
1974   Reelected to second term in Congress
1976   Spoke at Democratic National Convention in New York City; reelected to third term in Congress
1978   Retired from Congress; professor at University of Texas, Austin, Texas
1988   Spoke at Democratic National Convention in Atlanta, Georgia

INDEX

ABOUT THE AUTHOR

Naurice Roberts has written numerous stories and poems for children. Her background includes work as a copywriter, television personality, commercial announcer, college instructor, communications consultant, and human resources trainer. She received a B.A. in Broadcast Communications from Columbia College in Chicago, where she presently resides. *Barbara Jordan* is her second book published by Childrens Press.

6 50 5